Simple-to-Sew

NEEDLEPOINT

NEEDLEPOINT

Master new sewing skills with these
simple-to-make projects

HILARY MORE

B T Batsford Limited, London

First published in Great Britain by B. T. Batsford Ltd.
4 Fitzhardinge Street, London W1H 0AH

ISBN 0-7134-7926-4

A catalogue record for this book is available from
the British Library

This book was designed and produced by
Quintet Publishing Ltd.
6 Blundell Street
London N7 9BH

Creative Director: Richard Dewing
Designer: Isobel Gillan
Project Editor: Diana Steedman
Editor: Samantha Gray
Photographer: Andrew Sydenham
Illustrator: Terry Evans
Chart Illustrator: Jenny Dooge

Typeset in Great Britain by
Central Southern Typesetters, Eastbourne
Manufactured by Eray Scan Pte. Ltd., Singapore
Printed by Star Standard Industries (Pte.) Ltd., Singapore

ACKNOWLEDGEMENTS
The Publishers are grateful to the following
for their help with this publication:
Coats Craft UK, DMC Creative World Ltd, Paterna Persian Yarn,
Readicut Wool, Framecraft, Offray Ribbon, Jane Hibbert,
Sue Davies of Brethyn Brith, Jan Eaton, Beryl Miller,
Caroline Palmer, Dawn Marie Parmley, Angela Bartlett,
and to Creativity, Needlecraft Specialists,
45 New Oxford Street, London.

CONTENTS

INTRODUCTION

Welcome to the wonderful world of needlepoint! Needlepoint is embroidery worked in a variety of different yarns over a canvas background. Often called tapestry or canvaswork it appeals to all needleworkers as you can quickly create beautiful things for the home and family. Today this type of stitchery has broken away from its traditional past of complicated scenic designs worked in fine wool to embrace a collection of styles and techniques using wool, embroidery cotton, ribbon and fabric, in fact almost any type of yarn which can be used over canvas.

Needlepoint is simple and fun to do, and once you have mastered a few simple stitches you can create a host of patterns and designs. If you are a beginner, start with a simple project such as the Country Scene picture on page 20 – it's a perfect first-time project. At the other end of the scale, the sumptuous floral tieback on page 43 will delight a more experienced stitcher.

Before you begin read the following section on the materials and all the simple techniques you need to know. Then each of the projects comes complete with a chart, key and step-by-step instructions to help you produce a stunning piece of needlepoint.

Happy stitching!

MATERIALS AND EQUIPMENT

Canvas

Canvas is specifically made as the base for needlepoint. It is woven from stiffened cotton or linen and is generally available in white, buff or dark beige. Canvas is graded by the number of threads or holes to 1in/2.5cm. This is the mesh or gauge size – the smaller the number, the coarser the canvas. Choose the best quality canvas you can afford as this will provide a firm foundation on which to build your stitches and give the needlepoint a long life.

To work out how much canvas you need for a project, add an extra 3in/7.5cm all round for standard and large pieces and 2in/5cm for a small piece of work. This extra border of canvas allows for stretching and mounting. Canvas can be bought by the yard/metre or by the piece. The two main types of canvas are single or double thread canvas.

Single/mono canvas is woven with single crossing threads – horizontally and vertically. The best variety is interlock canvas, in which the threads are twisted and bonded together, providing a very firm background. Single canvas is easy to use, especially for a beginner, as any stitch can be worked over the even grid surface.

Double/Penelope canvas has pairs of crossing threads interwoven horizontally and vertically. The double threads can be gently parted and used as a single canvas to gain smoother curved lines and for areas of fine detailed work.

Rug canvas is a coarse interlock canvas which is available in a range of different widths.

Plastic canvas is bought in small sheets or pre-cut shapes such as circles, and is generally used for three-dimensional pieces of canvaswork. It is easy to cut and will not fray. Plastic canvas is a good choice for children learning to stitch.

Threads

Choose a thread appropriate to your needlepoint project and then match the thread to the type and size of canvas. It must be thick enough to completely cover the canvas, but the threaded needle must still be able to pass through the canvas mesh without pushing the threads apart and distorting the canvas. On large mesh canvas, several strands can be used together to cover the canvas threads. Buy all the yarn at the beginning of a project as dye lots can change and even a slight variation will show up, especially in a large area of one colour. Always work a test piece using your chosen thread on the chosen canvas to see how the finished piece will look.

Wool is the traditional yarn for needlepoint. Choose from tapestry, crewel and Persian wools. Once you are more experienced at stitching, you can try a range of different threads for experimental work, but use wool when you first begin to get the feel of needlepoint.

Tapestry wool is a firm, tightly twisted single 100% wool strand which cannot be divided. It is available in 11yd/10m skeins in a huge range of colours. Tapestry wool can also be bought in ¾oz/20g hanks (grounding wool) in a smaller range of popular background colours.

Crewel wool is a fine two-ply wool used for delicate canvaswork. It can be used as a single strand, or two, three, four or more strands can be used together on thicker canvases. Each colour is available in a wide range of shades, making this wool a good choice for detailed shading and ideal for blending different colours together to create muted shades.

Persian wool is slightly thicker than crewel wool. A loosely twisted three-strand wool, it can be divided or added to for working on different size canvas and to blend different colours together.

Stranded cotton is made up of six strands of lustrous mercerized cotton loosely twisted together. It can be used as a single strand or in groups – nine strands of stranded cotton is equal to a single strand of tapestry wool. Separate the six individual strands before regrouping into the number of threads needed for the project.

Soft embroidery cotton is a fairly thick twisted cotton thread with a matt finish. It is a successful alternative to tapestry wool for canvaswork.

Metallic threads are available in an extensive range of different thicknesses and shades, and small amounts can be mixed in or used over previously stitched sections.

Needles

Tapestry needles have rounded, blunt tips which do not split the yarn or the canvas threads. Their large eyes can accommodate different threads and thicker yarns. Needles are graded into size by thickness – the higher the number, the finer the needle.

As a quick guide: use a size 18 for 10- and 12-mesh canvas; size 20 for 14-mesh canvas; size 22 for 16- and 18-mesh canvas, and size 24 for fine 22- and 24-mesh canvases.

Frames

Mount the canvas in either a square or rectangular frame; there are two basic types:

Simple stretcher frames are made from two pairs of artists' stretchers. These are lengths of wood with mitred and slotted corners which can be quickly put together. The canvas is held on the frame with drawing pins.

Rotating frames are the most common of the frames. They come in a variety of sizes and are composed of two horizontal rollers slotted into two side pieces. Each roller has a strip of webbing stapled along one edge. The rollers are set into two straight side pieces and held firmly with four butterfly screws, one in each corner. These frames can be mounted on floor-standing supports, leaving both hands free for stitching.

Other Equipment Required

Scissors – use large dressmaking scissors for cutting canvas and a small, sharp-pointed pair for trimming and cutting yarn.

Floor-standing tapestry frames allow both hands to be free for stitching.

Thimble – if you normally wear a thimble for sewing, you'll find it useful when stitching tapestries to protect the middle (pushing) finger.

Masking tape – bind the raw canvas edges to protect the yarns and your hands.

Buttonhole thread, used in a sewing needle for lacing the canvas to a rotating frame and for holding the finished canvas over a backing board ready for framing.

Daylight bulb – fit this special type of light bulb in a side lamp to help you see the exact yarn colours during dark or gloomy days.

Tracing and graph paper are needed for designing and transferring designs. A thick, black, waterproof felt tip pen, ruler and set square are also useful for marking the canvas ready for stitching.

Firm board and drawing pins – when the finished piece of needlepoint is complete, pin the canvas over blotting paper to block the canvas back into shape.

TECHNIQUES

You don't need any special skills to work a piece of needlepoint. Once you have learnt a couple of basic stitches, you can create a masterpiece! Just use the following techniques as a guide to help you gain the best results:

Preparing the canvas

Cut canvas alongside a thread in both directions. To protect your hands and clothes from catching on the raw canvas and to prevent the edges from unravelling, cover with masking tape. Cut a length of 1in/25mm wide tape for each side and simply fold evenly in half over the canvas edges. Press the masking tape firmly in position.

Working in a frame

Unless you are working with plastic canvas or on a very small piece of canvas, it is advisable to stitch your canvas in a tapestry frame. It is a matter of preference, but if you learn to use a tapestry frame from the outset you will find it easier to work – both hands will be free – and you will gain an even result. A tapestry frame keeps the canvas stretched taut, making it easier to stitch in two movements – the correct way to work a piece of needlepoint – up through the canvas and back down again. With more experience you will find that you can stitch with a flowing rhythm, maintain an even tension and effect the minimum distortion to the canvas.

Fitting the canvas into a frame

1 Cut the canvas to the correct size for the project, at least 3in/7.5cm larger all round on standard and large projects and 2in/5cm larger all round on smaller pieces. Bind all edges with masking tape as shown.

2 Use a double length of contrasting sewing thread to tack across the canvas both lengthways and widthways to mark the centre of the canvas. Alternatively, use a permanent ink felt tip pen to mark the centre of the canvas on each side. Use a pencil to mark the centre of the webbing strips.

3 Turn under approximately ⅝in/1.5cm of canvas and, matching centre marks, oversew the canvas to the webbing along one roller. Repeat, to stitch the opposite edge of canvas to the row of webbing on the opposite roller. Begin stitching in the centre and work outwards to the edge on either side.

4 Assemble the frame. Wind any excess canvas round one of the rollers and tighten the screws to hold the canvas firm and taut.

5 To help support the side edges of the canvas, use buttonhole thread or fine string to lace the side edges of the canvas around the side sections of the frame.

Working from a chart

A needlepoint chart is made up of a grid of squares, with each square representing one stitch or one hole of canvas. Charts are not actual-size. In the materials list at the beginning of a project you'll find the canvas mesh size stated – buy this size of canvas to achieve the finished size of the project. To enlarge or reduce the size of the project, simply work over a finer canvas or over a canvas with a larger mesh count.

1 Mark the centre lines of the canvas – these will match up with the centre lines marked on the chart. To make it even easier to follow the chart, you can subdivide the canvas into ten square sections to match up with the heavier guide lines found on most charts. Count out the squares and mark across the canvas as before.
2 Each symbol or colour on a chart represents the colour and stitch with which that area is worked. Follow the key that goes with the chart and match the symbol or colour to the yarn colour, then work the number of stitches shown on the chart. Use the marked lines as a guide, removing them as soon as you have stitched over them.

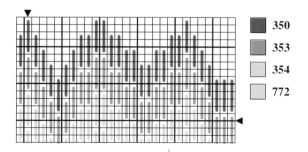

■	350
▨	353
□	354
□	772

Working from an actual-size design

Instead of using a chart, actual-size needlepoint designs can be marked on the canvas with a permanent ink felt tip pen or painted on to the canvas using waterproof paints. Mark out the outline before fitting the canvas into a tapestry frame.

1 If necessary, enlarge the design on a photocopier to the desired finished size. Go over the outline with a black felt tip pen so that you have a strong clear outline. Mark the centre of the design on each side.
2 Tape the design flat on a board. Matching centre marks, tape the canvas over the design. You will see the design through the canvas threads. Mark the outline on to the canvas, following the outline of the design. Make sure that the outline goes around the canvas holes to make it easier to follow when stitching.
3 Alternatively, use waterproof paints to paint the design on to the canvas in your chosen colours. Then you can match the areas to the wools when stitching.

Beginning to stitch

1 Cut approximately 18in/46cm of yarn. If the yarn is too long, the continuous rubbing against the canvas threads will make it fray and wear thin. Thread one end through a tapestry needle, wrapping the yarn tightly around the needle eye. Slide the yarn off the needle and thread through the eye. Knot the opposite end.
2 Take the threaded needle through the canvas, from the right side to the wrong side, leaving the knot ¾in/2cm in front of where the stitching will begin.

3 Bring the needle back to the right side of the canvas at the position for the first stitch. Work the first few stitches over the canvas and yarn end. When the knot is reached, cut it off and continue stitching.

4 Start new lengths of yarn by sliding the needle under the backs of a few worked stitches on the wrong side of the canvas, then bringing it through the correct hole to the right side ready for stitching.

5 To end a length of yarn, slide the needle under a few stitches at the back of the canvas. Trim off the end close to the canvas.

6 Try to avoid beginning and ending yarn lengths in the same place, row after row, as a ridge will form on the right side of the canvas.

Hints and tips for successful stitching

● Work each stitch in two movements, with the left hand on top of the canvas and the right hand underneath. Feed the needle up through the canvas to the right side and back down to the wrong side. You can only work this two-step method when the canvas is stretched taut in a tapestry frame. With practise, you will gain a flowing rhythm of stitching and maintain an even stitch tension with the minimum of canvas distortion.

● It is important to keep an even tension when stitching. Before you work any new stitch, practise on a spare piece of canvas to gauge the tension. If the stitches are too loose, they will not cover the canvas. If the stitches are too tight, the canvas will pucker and stretch out of shape.

● Try to come up through an empty hole of canvas and go down through the canvas in a partially filled hole. This will help to smooth down the yarn.

● The yarn will become twisted as you stitch – simply let the needle drop and the yarn will naturally untwist itself.

● Move the needle along the yarn as you stitch, to prevent the yarn from wearing thin where it is threaded through the needle eye.

● When stitching a tiny piece of canvas that cannot fit into a tapestry frame, place the canvas centrally on a spare piece of fabric and tack firmly together. Set the fabric in an embroidery hoop. Separate the rings; place the fabric over the smaller ring. Fit the larger ring over the top; press in place and tighten. Turn over and cut away the fabric from behind the canvas area – you can then stitch the canvas in the usual way.

Correcting mistakes

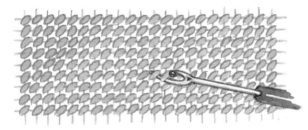

1 If you make a mistake, stitches can be quickly unpicked. Use a pair of small sharply-pointed scissors to snip through one stitch, then, using the blunt end of a tapestry needle, gently ease out the offending stitches. If you have a row of stitches to remove, use a seam ripper. Slide it just under the stitches on the wrong side to cut them. Re-stitch using a new length of yarn.

2 If you accidentally snip a canvas thread, a new piece of canvas can be grafted over the hole. Unpick the stitches surrounding the hole over a 1½in/4cm area. Cut a 1½in/4cm square of canvas with the same mesh count. Position the canvas square over the hole on the wrong side of the main canvas, match the canvas threads and tack in place. Now stitch over the area again in the usual way, working through both layers of canvas.

Blocking a piece of needlepoint

When you have finished a piece of needlepoint, you may find it has been pulled out of shape. Generally this can be cured by a steam press on the wrong side, while gently pulling the canvas back into shape. However, if the canvas is badly distorted, the best method is to stretch and block it back into shape.

1 Mark out the finished outline on a clean sheet of blotting paper and pin this over a clean, flat wooden board.

2 Dampen the back of the needlepoint using a wet sponge or plant water spray. The water is used just to soften the canvas, so do not over wet it.

3 Lay the canvas, right side up, over the board. Gently pull the canvas to match the outline of the needlepoint to the marked outline on the paper. Pin in place with drawing pins. Begin pinning at the centre top and work outwards, straighten the base edge to match and, finally, stretch and pin the sides in the same way. Use a set square to help check any right-angle corners. Space the drawing pins approximately 1in/2.5cm apart.

4 Check that the canvas is straight and leave to dry thoroughly for approximately 24 hours.

WELCOME TO SPRING

Finished size: 6 x 5in/15 x 12.5cm

This tiny springtime picture complete with gambolling lambs is worked entirely in half cross stitch using soft cottons over a 14 count canvas, so it's a good project for a beginner.

YOU WILL NEED

- 12 x 10in/30 x 25cm piece of white interlock tapestry canvas with 14 holes to 1in/2.5cm
- masking tape
- Anchor soft embroidery cotton in the following colours and amounts: two skeins of off white 2, one skein each of geranium 11, cornflower 147, grass green 242, almond green 260, dark almond green 262, canary yellow 288, black 403, beige 679, dusty pink 892 and kingfisher 9159
- tapestry needle, size 20
- tacking thread in contrasting colour
- tapestry frame
- picture frame and mounting board

1 To work To prevent the canvas edges from unravelling and to protect your hands and clothes, fold masking tape evenly in half over the raw canvas edges.

2 Using contrasting thread, tack across the canvas both lengthways and widthways to mark the centre (see Techniques, page 10).

3 Mount the canvas into the tapestry frame (see Techniques, page 10).

4 The chart shows the complete design for the picture. The centre is marked with black arrowheads – match these up with the lines of tacking stitches on the canvas. Each square on the chart represents one half cross stitch, worked over one canvas thread intersection.

5 Beginning in the centre, work the whole design in half cross stitch, following the chart and key.

Half cross stitch. Bring the needle out of the canvas and take a small diagonal stitch over one canvas thread intersection with the needle vertical, bringing it out of the canvas directly below. On the wrong side of the canvas the stitches will be vertical. Make sure that all the stitches slant in the same direction.

6 **To finish** When the needlepoint is complete, remove it from the tapestry frame. Peel off the masking tape from the canvas edges. Press the needlepoint on the wrong side over a damp cloth, gently pulling the canvas back into shape (see Techniques, page 13).

7 Remove the backing board from the frame and place the needlepoint centrally over it. Fix the needlepoint to the top edge of the board with a line of pins. Pull the canvas over the bottom edge of the board and hold in place with pins in the same way. Repeat on both sides.

8 Keep checking that the design is central and that the canvas is taut. Turn the board over to the wrong side and, using a double sewing thread, lace the two edges together from side to side and from top to bottom.

9 Remove the pins and replace the board inside the frame. Add another piece of card or board and tape across frame back to secure.

DECORATIVE ADDRESS BOOK

Finished size: to fit an address book 6⅛ x 4⅛in/15.5 x 10.5cm

This address book, with its delightful needlepoint cover, will inspire you to keep an up-to-date record of the addresses of your family and friends. Embroidered in tapestry wool over a 14 count canvas, the whole design is worked in traditional tent stitch.

YOU WILL NEED

- masking tape
- 16¼ x 12¼in/41 x 31cm piece of white single thread canvas with 14 holes to 1in/2.5cm
- black fine point felt-tip pen with permanent ink
- tacking thread in contrasting colour
- tapestry frame
- DMC tapestry wool in the following colours and amounts: 10 skeins of blue 7820, one skein each of orange 7947, purple 7708, red 7666, turquoise 7996, yellow 7973 and green 7911
- tapestry needle, size 20
- address book with a front face 4⅛ x 6⅛in/ 10.5 x 15.5cm and ½in/13mm thick spine
- 1yd/1m of ⅝in/15mm wide blue binding tape
- sewing thread to match binding

1 To work To protect your hands and clothes and the wool from catching on the canvas, fold masking tape evenly in half over the raw canvas edges.

2 Following the diagram and using the measurements of the address book, mark the outline of the cover centrally on the canvas with the felt tip pen. Mark ¾in/2cm deep pockets on either end of the cover. With a line of tacking stitches worked in a contrasting colour thread, mark the centre of the front cover section.

3 The chart shows the complete design for the front cover. The centre of the design is marked by arrowheads – match these up with the marked lines on the canvas. Each square on the chart represents one tent stitch worked over one canvas thread intersection.

4 Mount the canvas into the tapestry frame (see Techniques, page 10).

■	**7820**
■	**7947**
■	**7708**
■	**7666**
■	**7996**
■	**7973**
■	**7911**

Tent stitch. To work horizontal rows, bring the needle out of the canvas and take a small diagonal stitch over one canvas thread intersection. Take the needle down diagonally behind one horizontal and two vertical threads, then bring it out ready for the next stitch. On the wrong side, the stitches will be slightly longer diagonal stitches.

To work diagonally down the canvas, take the needle diagonally up over one canvas thread intersection then pass it vertically down behind two horizontal canvas threads.

To work diagonally up the canvas, the needle is passed horizontally behind two vertical canvas threads.

5 The design is worked in tent stitch throughout. Stitch the front cover following the chart and key. Then work the spine and back cover section in blue 7820 with odd stitches worked in turquoise 7996 and purple 7708 scattered around, in a similar way to the background of the front cover.

6 **To finish** Remove the completed needlepoint from the frame. Peel off the masking tape from the canvas edges. Press the needlepoint on the wrong side over a damp cloth, gently pulling the canvas back into shape.

7 Trim the canvas to within ⅜in/1cm of the needlepoint. Pin and stitch the binding along the edges of the needlepoint all round the cover. Mitre each corner and join binding edges together to fit.

8 Turn the binding at top and bottom edges to the inside and press well. Catch down the edge of the binding.

9 Turn in ¾in/2cm of needlepoint at each side to form pockets; press well. Catch down the pocket edges to the top and bottom of the cover to fix the pockets.

10 Insert the address book by slipping the cover ends inside the cover.

A COUNTRY SCENE

Finished size: approximately 7 x 6½in/18 x 16cm

Quick to stitch, this charming country scene is worked in long stitch over a 14 mesh canvas. Once the needlepoint stitches are completed, straight stitch, back stitch and French knots are added to bring character to this little picture.

YOU WILL NEED

- 11 x 10in/28 x 26cm piece of single canvas with 14 holes to 1in/2.5cm
- masking tape
- Anchor Tapisserie wool in the following shades: one skein each of white 8000, china blue 8624, laurel 9006, cornflower blue 8688, cathedral blue 8792, pale cornflower blue 8682, beige brown 9636, jade 8966, emerald 8988, spring green 9114, paprika 8240 and yellow/orange 8116
- Anchor stranded embroidery cotton: one skein of black 403
- tapestry needle, size 20
- crewel needle for embroidery details
- tapestry frame
- picture frame and backing board

1 **To work** To protect your hands and clothes and the wool from catching on the canvas, fold masking tape evenly in half over the raw canvas edges.

2 The chart shows the complete picture actual-size. Trace the design and mark it on to a clean sheet of paper, going over it with black felt tip pen. Tape the design flat, then tape the canvas centrally over the design. Use the felt tip pen to draw the design on to the canvas (see Techniques, page 11). Remove the tape and mount the canvas into the frame.

3 Work the picture following the chart and key for colours of the tapestry wools. The whole picture is worked in long satin stitch, working over a different number of canvas threads to completely fill each marked area.

4 When the needlepoint stitches are complete, embroider the smoke in back stitch using black embroidery cotton. Work a French knot in black embroidery cotton for each duck's eye and use yellow/orange 8116 to work the flowers along the river bank.

5 When the stitching is complete, remove the canvas from the frame. Press lightly on the wrong side over a damp cloth, gently pulling the canvas back into shape.

6 Frame the picture in the same way as for the Spring Picture (see page 16).

1	8000	5	8792	9	8988
2	8624	6	8682	10	9114
3	9006	7	9636	11	8240
4	8688	8	8966		

● 403 Stranded cotton – Back stitch

⬭ 8116 Tapisserie wool – Straight stitch

● 403 Stranded cotton – French knots

Long stitch. This stitch can be worked over a different number of canvas threads, depending on the area of the design. Always work in the same direction to keep an even tension.

Back stitch. Bring the needle out of the canvas and take a backward stitch, bringing the needle out the same distance in front of the first stitch. Then go into the first hole and out a stitch length in front. Keep repeating the same stitch.

French knots. Bring the cotton out of the canvas. Encircle the cotton twice with the needle. Holding the cotton firmly with the thumb twist the needle back into the canvas close to where it first emerged.

22

RIBBON RINGS

Finished size: approximately 6in/15cm in diameter

Brightly coloured fine ribbons are used to create napkin rings, being worked in Scottish stitch over a 7 mesh plastic canvas which provides a firm background.

YOU WILL NEED
(for four rings)

- 14 x 6in/35 x 15cm piece of plastic canvas with 7 holes to 1in/2.5cm
- fine felt tip pen with permanent ink
- 11yd/10m of ⅛in/3mm wide Offray Minidot ribbon in emerald
- 11yd/10m of ⅛in/3mm wide Offray Minidot ribbon in bright yellow
- tapestry needle, size 16
- 6 x 3in/15 x 8cm piece of felt in green and yellow
- fabric adhesive

1 **To work** Each chart shows the complete design for one napkin ring. Each background square on the chart represents one hole of canvas. The design is worked throughout in Scottish stitch, but with the central straight stitches worked in opposite directions.

2 Following the chart, count out the number of holes for each ring and use the felt tip pen to mark out the outlines for the four rings, leaving at least two empty holes between each ring.

3 Work two rings using the green ribbon for the tent stitch (see page 18) and the yellow ribbon for the centre slanted satin stitches; then work two rings in the reverse. Work each piece, following the chart and leaving the outer row of tent stitch unworked on each side edge.

4 When the needlepoint is complete, cut out each ring leaving a margin of one unworked canvas thread all round each piece.

5 Make up each ring in the same way. Fold the canvas into a ring. Work tent stitch over the two edges to join them; fasten off the ribbon securely. Then overcast around the top and bottom of the ring in either yellow or green ribbon, being careful to cover the edges of the canvas.

6 For each ring, cut a piece of felt 6 x 1½in/ 15 x 4cm. Using fabric adhesive, stick the felt centrally over the inside of each ring, butting edges together to neaten.

Scottish stitch. Work the slanted centre stitches first, working over one, two, three, four, three, two and one canvas thread. Work the next square of stitches in the opposite direction. Repeat, alternating the direction of the stitches. When the satin stitches are complete, outline the squares in tent stitch.

24

PUT YOUR FEET UP!

Finished size: to fit a stool pad 14 x 12in/36 x 30cm

Variegated wool is used to great effect on this stool top cover – the design includes just three shades of wool, but their changing hues provide a richness and variety of tone. The stool top cover is worked in straight Gobelin stitch over a 12 count canvas.

YOU WILL NEED

- masking tape
- 21 x 19in/54 x 50cm piece of white interlock tapestry canvas with 12 holes to 1in/2.5cm
- tapestry frame
- tacking thread in contrasting colour
- tapestry needle, size 18
- eight skeins of Brethyn Brith wool in water
- six skeins of Brethyn Brith wool in spring
- 12 skeins of Appletons wool in mid blue 156
- stool surround with padded top 14 x 12in/36 x 30cm

1 To work To protect your hands and clothes and prevent the wool from catching on the canvas, fold masking tape evenly in half over the raw canvas edges.

2 Tack across the canvas both lengthways and widthways to mark the centre.

3 Mount the canvas into the tapestry frame (see Techniques, page 10).

4 The chart shows just over one quarter of the design. The centre is marked with black arrowheads – match these up with the tacking stitches on the canvas.

5 The design mirror images vertically and horizontally along the centre lines.

6 The design is worked in straight Gobelin stitch over four canvas threads, with a straight stitch to mitre the blocks of stitches where they form a corner. Straight Gobelin stitch worked over two canvas threads is used to fill in where necessary around the edges.

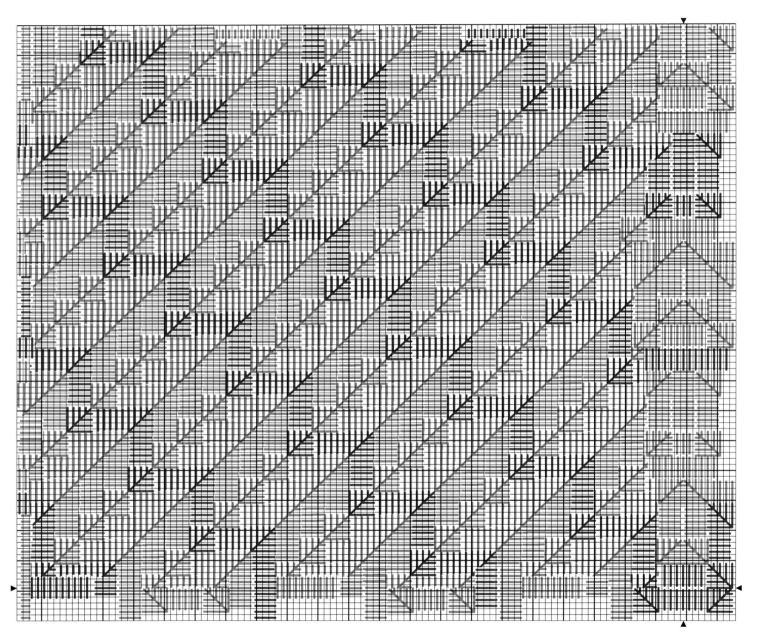

Mid Blue 156
Spring
Water

7 Work the first row out from the centre, counting carefully. Once this row is worked correctly, the whole pattern is set and each row can be worked alongside the previous one. Work the rows, alternating the three wool colours.

8 When the section shown is complete, work the remaining quarters in the same way.

9 **To finish** Remove the completed needlepoint from the frame. Peel off the masking tape and press on the wrong side over a damp cloth, gently pulling the canvas back into shape.

Straight Gobelin stitch. Bring the needle out of the canvas and insert four threads above. Bring the needle out to the left, ready for the second stitch. You can also work this stitch over two canvas threads to cover a smaller area.

11 Turn the pad over and, using a staple gun, fix the canvas firmly in place to the underside of the stool pad. Remove pins and replace stool pad into the stool surround.

10 Remove the stool pad from the surround. Place the needlepoint centrally over the pad and fold the surplus canvas to the back. Secure along the top edge with pins pushed into the pad. Pull the canvas taut over the opposite edge and secure with pins in the same way. Repeat at both side edges.

PICTURE IT

Finished size: 7¾ x 6⅜in/19.5 x 16cm

For a stunning photo or picture frame, work textured stitches in tapestry wool over a 10 count plastic canvas in this geometric design.

YOU WILL NEED

- two 7 x 8¾in/18 x 22cm pieces of plastic canvas with 10 holes to 1in/2.5cm plus two 1½ x 4¼in/4 x 11cm strips of canvas for the hinge
- DMC tapestry wool in the following colours and amounts: 10 skeins of dark blue 7247, one skein each of pale blue 7798, sea green 7952, pine green 7906, purple 7242 and fuchsia pink 7155
- tapestry frame
- tapestry needle, size 18
- black fine-point felt-tip pen with permanent ink
- thin card

1 To work For the frame front, mark the centre of one piece of plastic canvas both lengthways and widthways. The chart shows the complete design of the frame front. The centre of the design is marked with black arrowheads – match these up with the marked centre lines on the canvas.

2 Work the design from the chart centrally over the canvas, placing the colours and stitches as shown in the key, but omitting the two single green borders.

3 When the needlepoint is complete, cut out the front, leaving a margin of one unworked canvas thread all round the outer and inner (aperture) edge of the embroidery.

4 Work a row of overcast stitch around the inner (aperture) edge of the frame in pine green 7906.

5 Lay the front over the second piece of canvas, matching the canvas holes. Carefully draw round the outer edge of the front with felt pen to mark the outline of the frame back on the second piece of canvas. Cut a horizontal slit in the centre of the drawn rectangle on the back, making the slit 1⅝in/42mm across and approximately ⅛in/3mm deep.

6 Fill in the areas inside the drawn rectangle with reversed mosaic stitch (see page 30) worked in dark blue 7247, leaving a margin of one unworked canvas thread inside the edge of the rectangle and around the slit. Check that the worked area is exactly the same size and covers the same number of threads as the front. Now cut out the back, taking care to leave a margin of one unworked canvas thread around the edge.

7 Cover both strips of canvas with reversed mosaic stitch in dark blue 7247 to match the back. Leave one thread unworked around the outer edge.

8 To make the hinge, cut a strip of card 1¼ x 3½in/3 x 9cm. Sandwich the card strip between the two pieces of worked needlepoint, wrong sides together. Push the card down to one end. Overcast the two pieces together using dark blue 7247.

■	7247 RM
▨	7798 DL
□	7952 DL
▦	7906 WC
▨	7242 RM
▨	7155 C

RM: Reversed Mosaic

DL: Double Leviathan

WC: Woven Cross

C: Chequer

Reversed Mosaic stitch. Each block of this stitch is made up of a diagonal stitch worked over two vertical and two horizontal canvas threads at the centre of two short diagonal stitches. Work each block individually changing the slant of the stitches on alternate blocks.

Overcast stitch. This stitch is used to finish or join two pieces of plastic canvas. Work either from right to left or from left to right. Work diagonal stitches over the canvas edge. Take one stitch in each hole along a straight edge, but take two or three stitches in a hole on an inside or outside corner to ensure that you cover the canvas edge.

Woven Cross stitch. Work the blocks in horizontal rows. Begin with a large standard cross stitch over four vertical and four horizontal canvas threads. Overstitch the cross with four diagonal straight stitches, which should be woven over and under each other as they are stitched. Place each row of stitches directly above the previous row.

Chequer stitch. Work blocks of stitches over four vertical and four horizontal canvas threads. Alternate blocks of 16 tent stitches with blocks of diagonal stitches, making sure that all the stitches slant in the same direction.

Double Leviathan stitch. Start by working a large cross stitch over four vertical and four horizontal canvas threads. Then work a series of crossing stitches over the top, following the order shown here.

9 **Making up the frame** Push the end of the hinge without the card through the slit in the back panel until about ¼in/8mm protrudes on the wrong side. Secure the hinge firmly in place with several stitches.

10 Cut a 5⅝ x 7¼in/14.5 x 18.5cm piece of card. Lay the front embroidery over the card and mark the position of the aperture with a pencil. Centre the photograph or picture right side up over the pencil lines and secure with strips of masking tape.

11 Place the front and back together with wrong sides facing and slip the card in between. Overcast the front and back together with pine green 7906, taking care to fasten off the thread ends neatly.

BOX CLEVER

Finished size: to fit a trinket box with 3in/7.5cm lid

Keep all your trinkets and treasures in this pretty box decorated with a tiny beaded pansy. Worked over a 14 mesh canvas each stitch holds a bead offset by a stitched background of variegated embroidery cotton.

YOU WILL NEED

- 7in/18cm square of single thread interlock canvas with 14 holes to 1in/2.5cm
- masking tape
- one packet of glass seed beads in the following colours: dark purple, mauve, crimson, dark red and yellow
- Anchor stranded embroidery cotton in the following colours and amounts: one skein each of dark purple 102, mauve 100, dark red 45, crimson 59, yellow 291, variegated deep pink 1204
- circular elm trinket box with 3in/7.5cm diameter lid
- tapestry needle, size 20
- crewel needle, size 10
- fine point black felt tip pen with permanent ink
- tapestry frame

1 To work To protect your hands and clothes and the canvas from unravelling, fold the masking tape evenly in half over the raw canvas edges.

2 Trace the actual-size pansy on to a clean sheet of paper. Go over the outline with black felt tip pen.

3 Tape the paper flat, then tape the canvas centrally over the design. Draw the design on to the canvas using the felt tip pen.

4 Mount the canvas into the tapestry frame (see Techniques, page 10).

5 Work the pansy following the actual-size motif and key. Work the beaded areas in tent stitch using two strands of embroidery cotton in the crewel needle. Attach one bead with each stitch.

6 Stitch all the background in half cross stitch, using six strands of embroidery floss in the needle. Work the background up to the circular outline.

7 When the needlepoint is complete, carefully cut it out around the circular outline and fit inside the box lid, following the manufacturer's instructions.

■	102
■	100
■	45
■	59
▨	291
□	1204

Half cross stitch. Bring the needle out of the canvas and take a small diagonal stitch over one canvas thread intersection with the needle vertical, bringing it out of the canvas directly below. On the wrong side of the canvas the stitches will be vertical. Make sure that all the stitches slant in the same direction. When working with beads, bring the needle out of the canvas, pick up one bead and take the needle back down into the canvas. The beads will slant in the opposite direction to the stitches.

BE MINE

Finished size: approximately 14in/35cm square

This unusual cushion is worked in a variety of stitches over a 10 mesh canvas. Each square is worked in a different stitch and outlined in tent stitch, and tassels at each corner of the cushion are the perfect finish.

YOU WILL NEED

- 18in/45cm square of white single thread canvas with 10 threads to 1in/2.5cm
- masking tape
- tacking thread in contrasting colour
- tapestry needle, size 18
- tapestry frame
- DMC tapestry wools in the following colours and amounts: seven skeins of blue 7318, five skeins each of pink 7804 and blue 7319, four skeins each of blue 7314 and white, three skeins of pink 7708, two skeins of pink 7600 and one skein of yellow 7726
- 16in/40cm square of fabric for backing
- matching sewing thread
- 12in/30cm zip
- 14in/35cm square cushion pad
- 1¾yd/1.5m of cord
- four tassels or four skeins of DMC tapestry wool of blue 7318

1 To work To protect your hands and clothes and the wool from catching on the canvas edges, fold masking tape evenly in half over the raw canvas edges.

2 Tack lengthways and widthways across the canvas using a contrasting sewing thread to mark the centre (see Techniques, page 10).

3 The chart shows the complete design for the cushion. The centre is marked by black arrowheads which must match up with the tacking stitches on the canvas. Each background square on the chart represents one hole of canvas.

4 From the centre count out the holes and mark the squares that make up the design.

5 Fit the canvas into the tapestry frame (see Techniques, page 10).

6 The design is worked in a variety of needlepoint stitches. Work the design following the chart for the stitches and the key for the wool colours. Begin by working the central heart and square in velvet and diagonal mosaic stitch, then outline each of the remaining squares with a row of tent stitches (see page 18).

7 Fill in each square with the appropriate needlepoint stitch. In some cases the stitches on the outside of each square will have to be shortened to fill the area.

8 When the design is complete, remove the canvas from the frame. Peel off the masking tape. Press gently on the wrong side over a damp cloth, gently pulling the canvas back into shape (see Techniques, page 13).

rice	byzantine	slanted gobelin	rice
cross	velvet		cross
slanted gobelin	hungarian / diagonal mosaic		slanted gobelin
rice	cross	cashmere	rice

☐ white ☐ 7314 ☐ 7318 ☐ 7319 ☐ 7600 ☐ 7708 ☐ 7726 ☐ 7804

9 For the back cut two pieces of fabric, 15 x 8¼in/38 x 20.5cm. Place right sides together, and pin and tack across the centre. Stitch in from each side, leaving a 12in/30cm central opening; press seam open.

10 Place zip face down over the tacked section of the seam; pin and tack. Turn fabric over and, with a piping foot on the machine, stitch round zip; partially open zip.

11 Place back and front right sides together; pin and stitch all round. Trim and turn right side out through zip. Insert cushion pad and close zip.

12 Handsew cord round outer edge, slotting ends neatly into seam. Add tassels. To make tassels, cut two short lengths of wool; tie one around a skein 1¼in/3cm from top. Slot second length through top loop and tie. Remove skein bands. Trim tassel to 5½in/13cm.

Byzantine stitch. Work satin stitches diagonally over four vertical and four horizontal canvas threads. This creates a woven, step effect.

Velvet stitch. This stitch is worked upwards from left to right. Bring the needle out of the canvas and insert two threads up and two threads to the right. Bring the needle out again at the first hole and hold down a loop of yarn while taking a vertical stitch. Take the final stitch over the canvas forming a cross with the first stitch. When the rows are complete cut and trim the loops.

Cross stitch. Bring the needle out of the canvas, and take a stitch two threads to the left and two threads up to form the half-cross. Complete the crosses working in the opposite direction.

Cashmere stitch. Work diagonal stitches in sequence over one, two and two canvas intersections, with the lower end of each stitch falling exactly beneath the other and with each set of three stitches moving one thread to the right each time when working diagonally downwards. When working upwards from right to left, move the three stitches one thread to the left.

Hungarian stitch. This stitch can be worked in one or two different colours. Take vertical straight stitches over two, four and two horizontal threads of canvas, leaving two vertical threads between each group of stitches. Fit each row alternately into the preceding row.

Slanted Gobelin. This stitch can be worked from right to left or from left to right. Work each stitch over two horizontal and one vertical canvas threads.

Diagonal Mosaic stitch. Work down the canvas from left to right and then up again. Work over one, two and one canvas thread. Fit the next row so the short stitches are next to the long stitches.

Rice stitch. First cover the area with cross stitch worked over four canvas threads, then work a small diagonal stitch over each corner of the cross stitch over two canvas threads.

MAGIC CARPET

Finished size: 39½ x 28in/100 x 72cm

Turn ragged fabric strips into a woven carpet by working Parisian stitch over a rug canvas. The alternate rows of two cotton fabrics will create a smart, hardwearing rug.

YOU WILL NEED

- 4½yd/4m of 45in/115cm wide cotton fabric, such as Madras, in two different designs
- rotary cutter
- 46 x 28in/117 x 72cm piece of rug canvas with 3⅓ holes to 1in/2.5cm
- bodkin needle
- 3¾yd/3.5m No.6 piping cord

1 **To work** To prepare the fabric strips, cut out 1⅜in/3.5cm wide strips from across the fabric.

2 Lay the canvas on the table with the selvedges on either side. Place a heavy object on the canvas end to prevent it slipping.

3 Count up the first eight rows; fold the canvas along the eighth row to the right side. Leaving two holes free, work the first few rows through both thicknesses of canvas.

4 Work each row in Parisian stitch, but take the long stitches over eight threads and the short stitches over four threads of canvas. Alternate the two fabrics row by row.

5 Neaten all the fabric ends by running them through a few stitches on the wrong side when beginning a new length or ending a length of fabric.

6 Work across the canvas until you reach the last 16 rows, then turn the canvas up and work the final rows through double canvas in the same way as before.

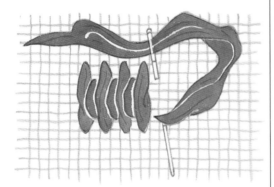

Parisian stitch. Work from left to right, bring the fabric through the canvas and insert the needle eight threads above, bringing the needle out six threads down and one thread to the right. To make the short stitches, insert the needle four threads up and come out six threads down and one thread to the right ready for the next long stitch.

7 To neaten the edge, fold piping cord inside a fabric strip and lay along outer edge of rug. Overcast over the piping, turning under raw edge of strip and overlap the stitches.

FLORENTINE NEEDLECASE

Finished size: 4¾ x 3½in/12 x 8cm

Worked in traditional Florentine stitch, this pretty needlecase will be a bonus for any sewing box. Use stranded wool and work over a 12 mesh canvas, then add felt leaves and complete with a twisted wool edge.

YOU WILL NEED

- 10 x 8½in/26 x 22cm piece of single thread canvas with 12 holes to 1in/2.5cm
- masking tape
- tacking thread in contrasting colour
- tapestry needle, size 18
- tapestry frame
- Paterna Persian wool in the following colours and amounts: one skein each of dark pink 350, medium pink 353, pale pink 354 and yellow 772
- 8 x 6in/20 x 15cm piece of cotton fabric for lining
- sewing thread to match lining fabric
- 5½ x 4¾in/14 x 12cm piece of pink felt
- 5 x 4¼in/13 x 11cm piece of yellow felt
- pinking shears

1 **To work** To protect your hands and clothes and the wool from catching on the canvas edges, fold masking tape evenly in half over the raw canvas edges.

2 Tack both lengthways and widthways across the canvas using a contrasting sewing thread to mark the centre (see Techniques, Page 10). Now mark the outline of the needlecase, 6½ x 4¾in/16 x 12cm, on to the canvas.

3 Mount the canvas into the tapestry frame (see Techniques, page 10).

4 The chart shows the rows of Florentine stitch that are worked in rows across the needlecase. The centre is marked with black arrowheads which must match the tacking stitches on the canvas. Each background square on the chart represents one hole of canvas. Repeat the rows working the colours in order.

5 Work the first row across the centre of the canvas using dark pink 350 to set the pattern working each stitch over four canvas threads. Then work each row in the same way above and below the first row, working the rows in colour order, until the whole area is filled. At the side edges some stitches will have to be shortened to fill the gaps.

6 When the needlepoint is complete, remove it from the frame. Peel off the masking tape and press lightly on the wrong side over a damp cloth, gently pulling the canvas back into shape.

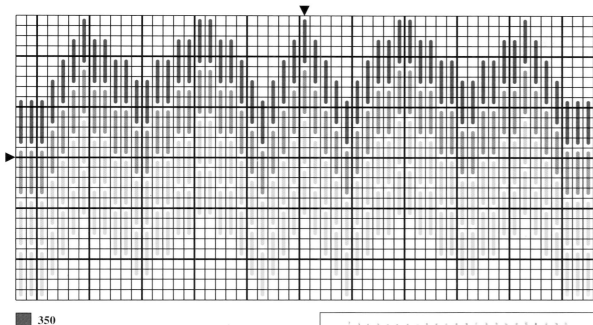

■	350
■	353
□	354
□	772

7 Place the canvas on to the lining with right sides facing; pin and stitch against the stitched area all round, leaving an opening in one side. Trim off corners and across seams and turn right side out. Close opening; press again.

Florentine stitch. This stitch is used for working Florentine patterns, with two or more colours forming a wave design. The size of the wave will vary depending upon the number of stitches or the number of threads over which the stitches are worked.

8 Using pinking shears, trim the two pieces of felt for the inner leaves. Lay the leaves centrally one on top of the other and position centrally on to the lining side of the needlecase. Hand sew the leaves in place by stitching down the centre.

9 Measure round the outer edge of needlecase. Cut six strands each of pink 350 and yellow 772 to three times this length. Tie ends together. Slot one end over a door handle. Slide a pencil into opposite loop. Keep turning the pencil to twist the wool. When tightly twisted, remove from handle and hold ends together while wool twists together to form a cord. Handsew round case, neatening the ends.

FABULOUS FLORALS

Finished size: approximately 28½ x 4¾in/72 x 12cm

YOU WILL NEED
(for one pair of tiebacks)

- 20 x 40in/50 x 100cm piece of white single interlock tapestry canvas with 12 holes to 1in/2.5cm
- masking tape
- tacking thread in contrasting colour
- tapestry needle, size 20
- DMC tapestry wool in the following colours: 22 skeins of ecru, four skeins each of dusky pink 7204, dark dusky pink 7205, pale rose 7132, medium rose 7760, dark rose 7759, pale green 7369, grey/green 7394, olive green 7396, dark olive green 7398, three skeins each of crimson 7212, deep rose 7758, yellow ochre 7504, two skeins each of mid crimson 7210, sea green 7326, dark sea green 7327, yellow/brown 7505, brown 7508, mauve 7896, deep purple 7228, one skein of grey/blue 7323 and deep mauve 7255
- tapestry frame
- 32 x 16in/80 x 40cm piece of cotton fabric for lining
- 30 x 11in/75 x 28cm piece of interfacing
- 4½yd/4m of insertion cord
- sewing thread to match lining fabric
- four ½in/13mm diameter curtain rings

old back your curtains in style with this pretty flower-strewn tieback. Worked in tapestry wool over a 12 mesh canvas, this beautiful addition to your home furnishings will last a lifetime.

1 **To work** To protect your hands and clothes and the wool from catching on the edge, fold masking tape evenly in half over the raw canvas edges.

2 Tack both lengthways and widthways across the canvas using a contrasting thread to mark the centre (see Techniques, page 10). Both tiebacks can be worked one above the other with a gap of about 2¾in/7cm between them.

3 Mount the canvas into the tapestry frame (see Techniques, page 10).

4 The chart shows the right-hand side of one tieback with the centre marked by black arrowheads which must match up with the tacking threads on the canvas. Each background square on the chart represents one tent stitch worked over one intersection of canvas. To complete the left-hand side of the tieback reverse the section shown and work from the centre outwards.

5 Work the design throughout in tent stitch, following the chart and key for colours. Begin by stitching the flowers, leaves and other motifs across the whole tieback, then fill in the background in ecru.

Tent stitch. To work horizontal rows, bring the needle out of the canvas and take a small diagonal stitch over one canvas thread intersection. Take the needle down diagonally behind one horizontal and two vertical threads, then bring it out ready for the next stitch. On the wrong side, the stitches will be slightly longer diagonal stitches.

To work diagonally down the canvas, take the needle diagonally up over one canvas thread intersection then pass it vertically down behind two horizontal canvas threads.

To work diagonally up the canvas, the stitches are worked in the same way but the needle is passed horizontally behind two vertical threads.

6 When the needlepoint is complete, remove it from the frame. Peel off the masking tape and press on the wrong side over a damp cloth, gently pulling the canvas back into shape.

7 Cut out each needlepoint piece, leaving a ⅝in/1.5cm border all round. Use the needlepoint as a template to cut one piece from the lining and one piece from the interfacing to the same size.

8 Place the interfacing on to the wrong side of needlepoint, catching together around the outside edge. Pin the cord around needlepoint, on the right side, with the cord facing inwards and edges matching. Join ends together to fit.

9 Place lining fabric on to the needlepoint with right sides facing; pin and stitch against the needlepoint all round, leaving an opening in one side. Trim and turn right side out. Turn in opening edges and slipstitch to close.

10 Hand sew a curtain ring to both ends of the tieback.

■	7212	■ 7759	□ 7369	□ 7505		
■	7210	■ 7758	■ 7228	■ 7508		
■	7205	■ 7398	■ 7255	□ 7323		
■	7204	■ 7396	■ 7896	■ 7326		
■	7132	■ 7394	□ 7504	■ 7327		
■	7760	□ ecru				

BELT AND BUTTONS

Finished size: Belt: 25 x 1½in/63.5 x 4cm Buttons: 1¼in/29mm diameter

Stitch a matching pair of smart self-covered buttons and belt for a child. Worked in coton perle in cross-cornered cushion stitch, choose colours to suit the outfit.

YOU WILL NEED

- belt: 29 x 5½in/74 x 14cm piece of white interlock tapestry canvas with 14 holes to 1in/2.5cm
- buttons: 8½in/22cm square of white interlock tapestry canvas with 14 holes to 1in/2.5cm
- masking tape
- DMC coton perle no 5 in the following colours and amounts: two skeins of navy 939, one skein each of green 502, orange 742, mauve 208, red 321, pink 893 and blue 792
- tapestry needle size 20
- tapestry frame
- 26 x 2¾in/66 x 7cm piece of navy blue cotton fabric
- 25 x 1½in/63.5 x 4cm piece of medium-weight iron-on interfacing
- tacking thread
- three hook and eye fasteners
- Newey Rimit self-covering buttons, 1¼in/29mm in diameter

1 **To work the belt** To prevent the canvas edges from unravelling and to protect your hands and clothes, fold masking tape evenly in half over the raw canvas edges.

2 Mount the canvas into the tapestry frame (see Techniques, page 10).

3 The chart shows a section of the design, which is repeated across the canvas. Each square on the chart represents one hole of canvas.

4 Beginning 2in/5cm in from one short edge, work an outline of tent stitch (see page 18) centrally across the canvas in navy 939 following the chart.

5 Fill in the spaces with cross-cornered cushion stitch using the remaining six coloured embroidery threads randomly.

6 To complete the belt work a row of plait stitch all round the outer edge in navy 939.

7 **To finish** Remove the completed needlepoint from the frame. Peel off the masking tape from the canvas edges. Press the needlepoint on the wrong side over a damp cloth, gently pulling the canvas back into shape.

8 Turn in all edges along the line of the needlepoint and press. Trim raw canvas edges as necessary.

9 Fuse the interfacing centrally to wrong side of fabric strip. Turn in raw edges of fabric strip for ⅝in/1.5cm. Place strip to needlepoint belt with wrong sides facing. Slipstitch the fabric to the needlepoint all round the outer edge.

10 Handsew three hooks and eyes to short edges so belt edges butt neatly together.

792   742   321   939

502   208   893

Plait stitch. Bring the needle out of the canvas (A) and insert four threads to the right and four threads up (B), coming out of the canvas directly below (C), forming a diagonal stitch. Insert the needle at (D), four threads up and two threads left, bringing the needle out directly below (E). Keep working in the same way across the canvas.

Cross-cornered cushion stitch. The stitch is worked over six vertical and six horizontal canvas threads. Begin at one corner of the square and work over one, two, three, four, five, six, five, four, three, two and one canvas thread intersections to cover the square. Then bring the needle up at the opposite corner and work diagonal stitches across half the square again working in the opposite direction. The squares can be arranged together in different ways to form a further pattern.

11 **Buttons** Divide the canvas equally into four with contrasting thread. Work one four-square pattern in the centre of each canvas section, working with random colours, in the same way as for the belt.

12 Cut out and fit the canvas into a button mould following manufacturers' instructions.